THE

JEWISH QUESTION COLLECTION

MORE THAN 300 QUESTIONS ABOUT

THE BIBLE

HOLIDAYS

HISTORY

PEOPLE AND PLACES

CUSTOMS

Written by Linda Schwartz • Illustrated by Ronni Wyner

The Learning Works

Text Design & Editorial Production: Kimberley A. Clark

Cover Illustration: Beverly Armstrong

Copyright © 1994—Linda Schwartz
THE LEARNING WORKS, INC.
P.O. Box 6187
Santa Barbara, CA 93160
All rights reserved.
Printed in the United States of America.

Library of Congress Number: 93-080430
ISBN: 0-88160-247-7

Dedicated to
Stephen and Michael
with love.

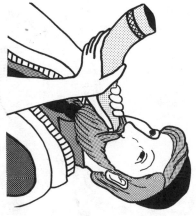

Introduction

This book is a collection of more than three hundred questions on basic Judaism covering topics such as history, holidays, Bible stories, rituals, and more. It is intended for use in the religious classroom, at home, or anywhere children have empty minutes to fill. This book is ideal to use on rainy days, before religious school recess, while traveling, or for holiday and family get-togethers.

The questions have been placed two to a page. Questions on any one page cover different topics but are of a similar degree of difficulty. The book has been arranged so that the questions progress from easy through medium to hard.

No collection of questions would be complete without a collection of answers. In this book, answers appear on pages 158–176. They have been listed by page number and keyed by letter to the question's position on the page. Thus, answer **a** is for the question on the left side of the page, and answer **b** is for the question on the right side of the page.

The Jewish Question Collection
© 1994—The Learning Works, Inc.

3

A Special Message to Teachers

There are numerous ways to use this book in your religious school classroom. To begin with, you can open it to pages appropriate to your grade level and ask your students a few questions to start your day or to fill in those last minutes before recess or dismissal. You can also turn the questions into a self-checking game. Select pages on which the questions are appropriate for the grade level you teach. Duplicate some of these pages and cut the questions apart. Glue each question to one side of a plain 4" x 6" index card. Glue or write the corresponding answer on the other side of the card. Laminate the cards and make them available at a classroom learning center.

In addition, you can use these questions for question bees, for staged classroom quiz shows that follow a radio or television format, as classroom motivators, or as assignments to reinforce research skills.

In short, you may find that *The Jewish Question Collection* provides a lot of answers for a busy religious school teacher in a bustling classroom.

A Special Message to Parents

The ways to use this book are almost endless. To begin with, *The Jewish Question Collection* is perfect for filling time on rainy days, using as a holiday or party game, or making the miles go faster when you travel. This book is great for dinner-time quizzes the whole family can enjoy. The questions in the front of the book are ideal for the younger children in your family and those in the middle are suitable for older kids. Teenagers and adults will be challenged by the questions that appear in the back section of the book. If your child does not know an answer, have him or her look it up in a dictionary, encyclopedia, or Jewish reference book. *The Jewish Question Collection* is not only educational, it's fun for the entire family!

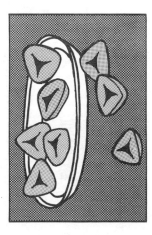

The Jewish Question Collection
© 1994—The Learning Works, Inc.

Acknowledgments

Special thanks to my young havurah helpers: Deborah and Jonathan Bialis, Sarah Brennan, Beth Presser, and Allyson Toscher. My appreciation to Rabbi Richard J. Shapiro, Congregation B'nai B'rith, Santa Barbara, California; Rae Aronoff, Lois and Carl Conn, Dovid Moshe ben Tzvi, Joel Block, and Phyllis and Kate Amerikaner for critiquing the manuscript. Many thanks to Kim Clark and Diane Namm for their editing expertise, to Ronni Wyner for illustrating the book, and to Beverly Armstrong for the cover design.

What is the name of the top spun during Hanukkah?

How many points are on the Star of David?

The Jewish Question Collection
© 1994—The Learning Works, Inc.

What is
the Jewish day
of rest
called?

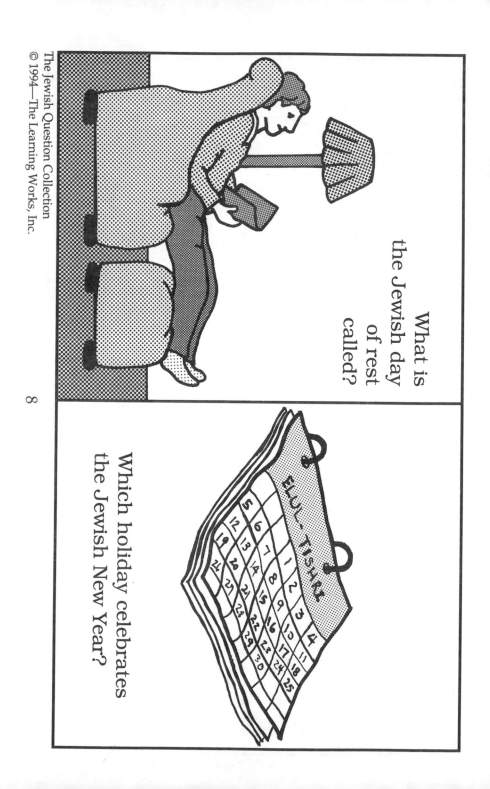

Which holiday celebrates
the Jewish New Year?

ELUL — TISHRI

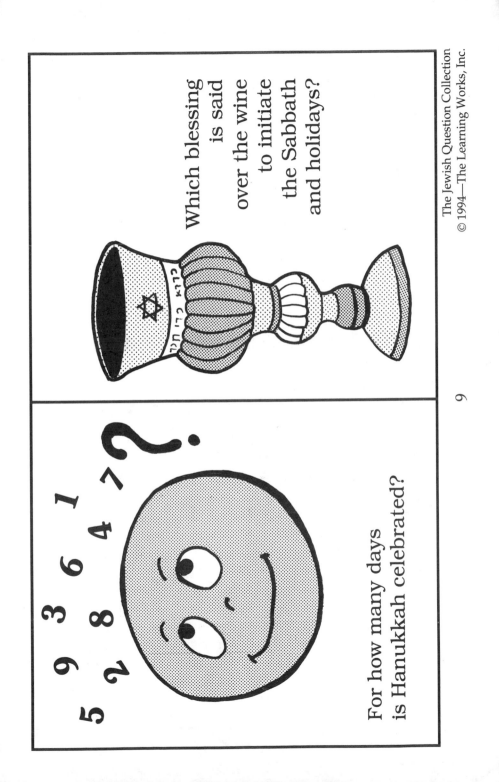

Which blessing
is said
over the wine
to initiate
the Sabbath
and holidays?

For how many days
is Hanukkah celebrated?

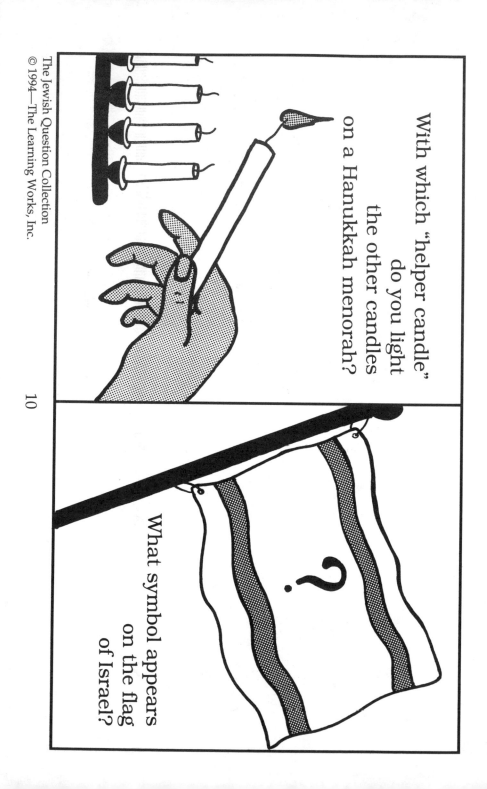

With which "helper candle"
do you light
the other candles
on a Hanukkah menorah?

What symbol appears
on the flag
of Israel?

In which garden did Adam and Eve live?

What is the name of the ram's horn blown on Rosh Hashanah?

The Jewish Question Collection
© 1994—The Learning Works, Inc.

What do you call the skullcaps worn in synagogue?

On which holiday do Jews fast and ask for forgiveness?

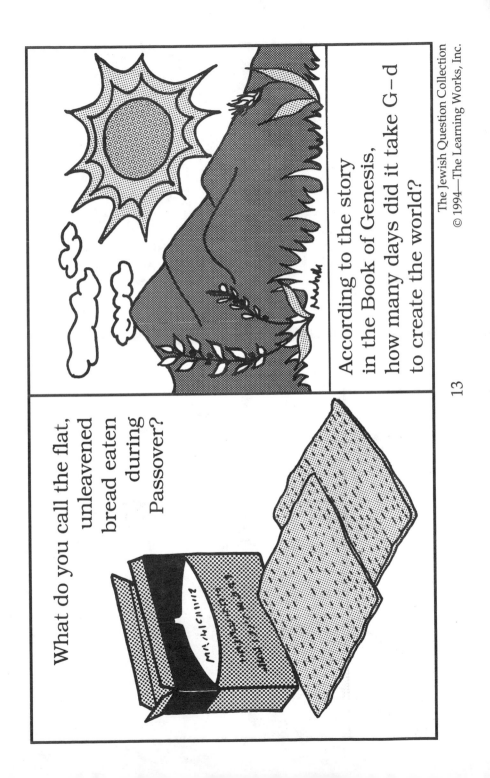

What do you call the flat, unleavened bread eaten during Passover?

According to the story in the Book of Genesis, how many days did it take G–d to create the world?

The Jewish Question Collection
© 1994—The Learning Works, Inc.

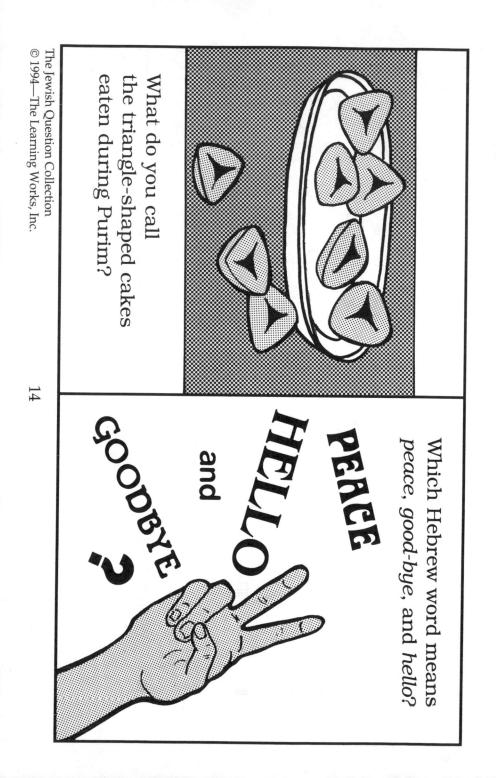

What do you call the triangle-shaped cakes eaten during Purim?

Which Hebrew word means *peace, good-bye,* and *hello?*

PEACE
HELLO
and
GOODBYE?

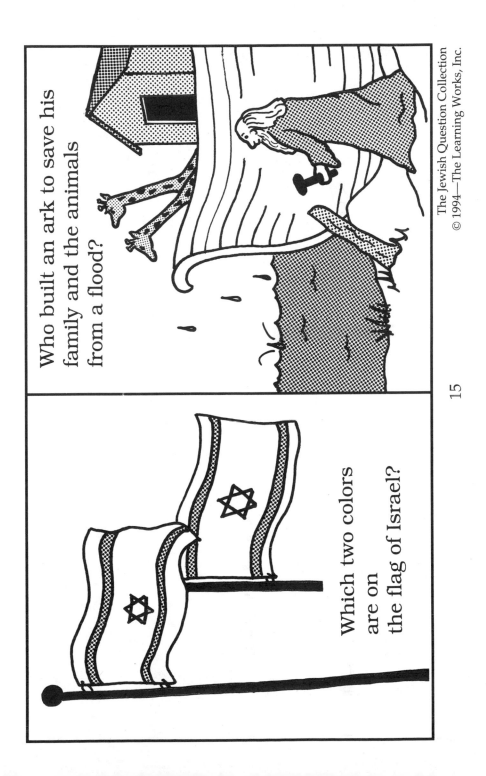

Who built an ark to save his family and the animals from a flood?

Which two colors are on the flag of Israel?

15

The Jewish Question Collection
© 1994—The Learning Works, Inc.

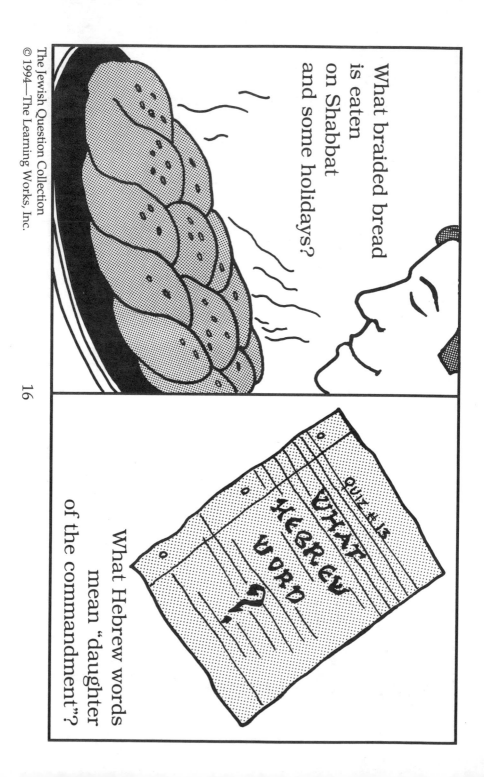

What braided bread
is eaten
on Shabbat
and some holidays?

What Hebrew words
mean "daughter
of the commandment"?

The Jewish Question Collection

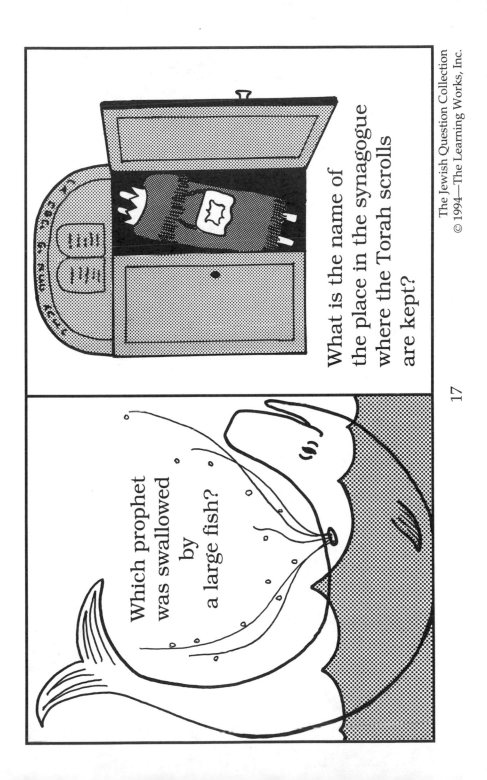

What is the name of
the place in the synagogue
where the Torah scrolls
are kept?

Which prophet
was swallowed
by
a large fish?

The Jewish Question Collection
© 1994—The Learning Works, Inc.

On which holiday is the Megillah of Esther read?

Who was the young shepherd who killed a giant named Goliath?

What is the main ingredient in latkes?

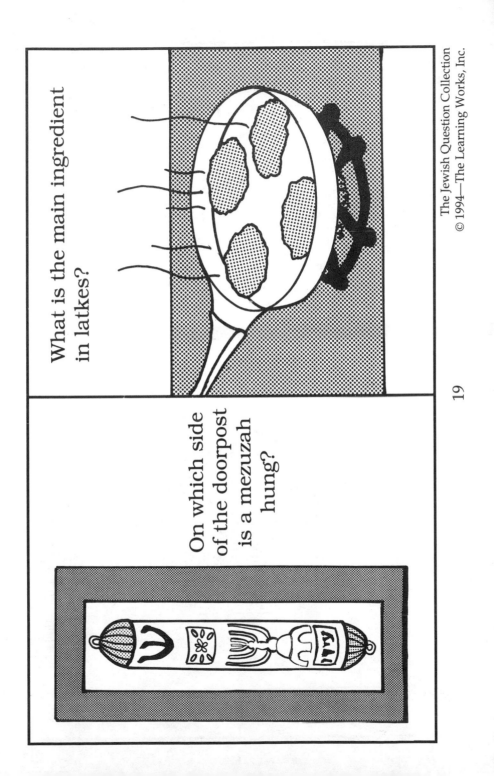

On which side of the doorpost is a mezuzah hung?

The Jewish Question Collection
© 1994—The Learning Works, Inc.

To what does *kashrut* refer:
dietary laws, books of the Torah,
or ceremonial candles?

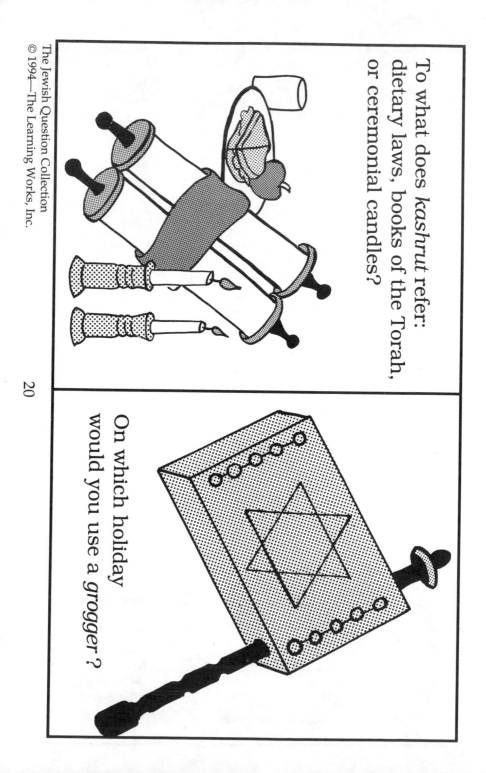

On which holiday
would you use a *grogger*?

In the story of Jewish slavery in Egypt, how many plagues did the Egyptians suffer?

To whom did G–d speak from a burning bush?

On which holiday
is the *afikoman* hidden?

What did G–d do
on the seventh day of creation?

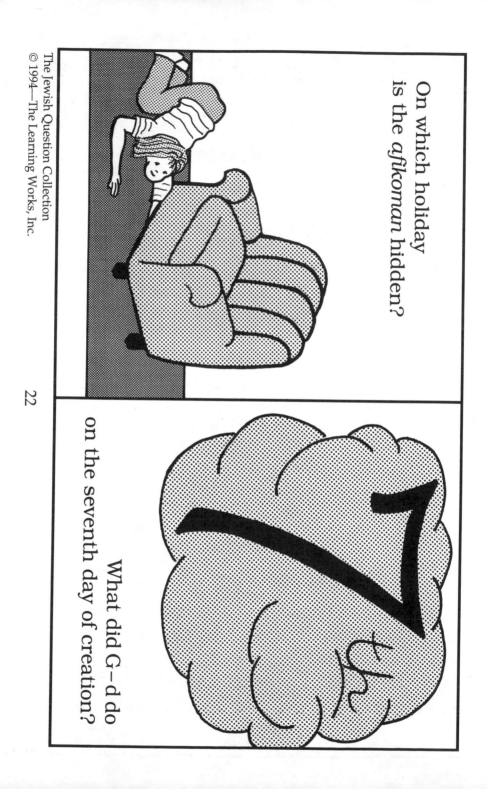

In what direction
is Hebrew
read and written?

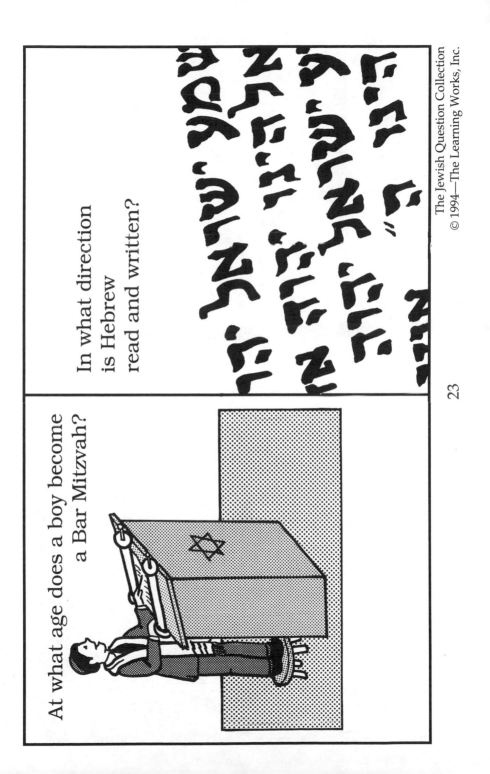

At what age does a boy become
a Bar Mitzvah?

The Jewish Question Collection
© 1994—The Learning Works, Inc.

What was the departure of Moses and the Israelites from Egypt called?

Which holiday comes from the Hebrew word meaning booths or huts?

Is a *tallit* a hat, a prayer shawl, or food on the seder plate?

How many questions does the youngest child ask during a Passover seder?

The Jewish Question Collection
© 1994—The Learning Works, Inc.

According to
the Torah,
who offered
his son to G–d
as a sacrifice?

אבגד

What is the first letter
of the
Hebrew alphabet?

The Jewish Question Collection
© 1994—The Learning Works, Inc.

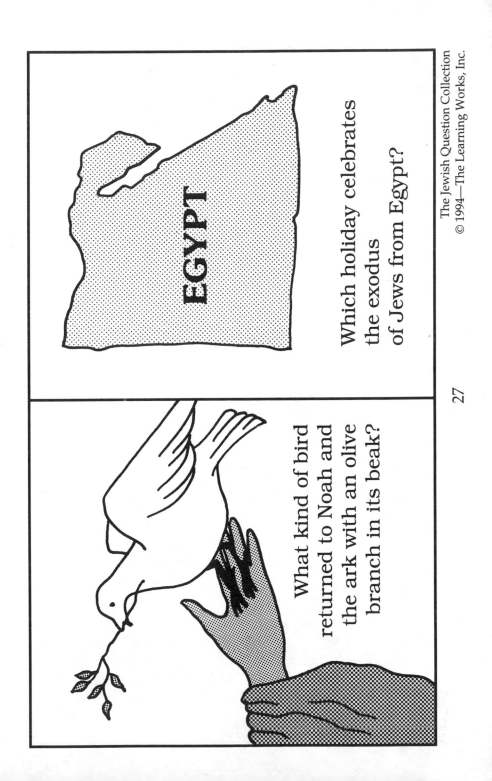

Which holiday celebrates
the exodus
of Jews from Egypt?

EGYPT

What kind of bird
returned to Noah and
the ark with an olive
branch in its beak?

27

The Jewish Question Collection
© 1994—The Learning Works, Inc.

Why do people stand when the ark that holds the Torah is opened?

Who was the first-born son of Adam and Eve?

29

The Jewish Question Collection
© 1994—The Learning Works, Inc.

Where did Moses receive
the Ten Commandments?

How long does it
take to read
the entire Torah,
when it is read during
regular weekly services?

Who was given a coat of many colors by his father, Jacob?

Who had his hair cut by Delilah while he slept?

The Jewish Question Collection
© 1994—The Learning Works, Inc.

On the seder plate, which item symbolizes the ancient sacrifices in the Temple?

On which holiday do children dress in costumes and celebrate the rescue of Persian Jews?

On Rosh Hashanah, what are apples and challah dipped into as a symbol of hope for a sweet New Year?

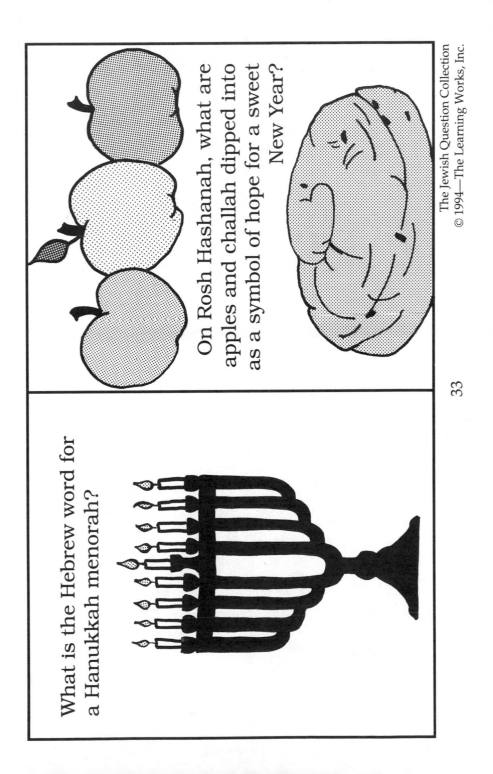

The Jewish Question Collection
© 1994—The Learning Works, Inc.

What is the Hebrew word for a Hanukkah menorah?

At a Passover seder, why are green vegetables, or *karpas*, dipped in salt water?

What was the name of Adam and Eve's second son?

JOSEPH ESAU

SAMSON

JACOB CAIN ISAAC

ENOCH

In Reform and Conservative temples, what ceremony takes place when boys and girls are in the tenth grade?

What is the second letter of the Hebrew alphabet?

The Jewish Question Collection
© 1994—The Learning Works, Inc.

Which is *not* a part of the Havdalah service: wine, menorahs, spices, or candles?

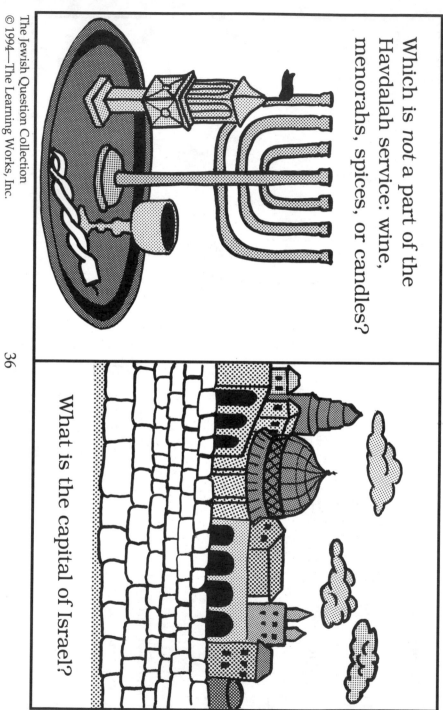

What is the capital of Israel?

What happens when the dreidel lands on the Hebrew letter *hay?*

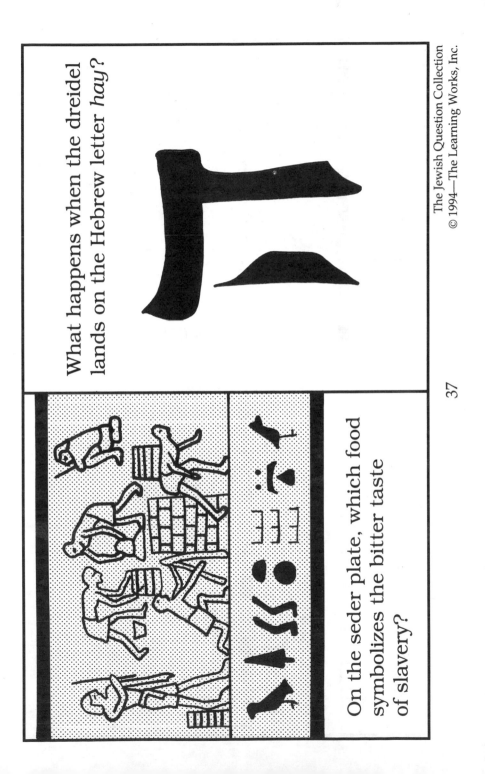

On the seder plate, which food symbolizes the bitter taste of slavery?

The Jewish Question Collection
© 1994—The Learning Works, Inc.

What is a *minyan*?

Which sea is the saltiest
in the world?

Would you wear, eat, or plant *tzimmes?*

Are Torahs written by hand, produced on computers, or typewritten?

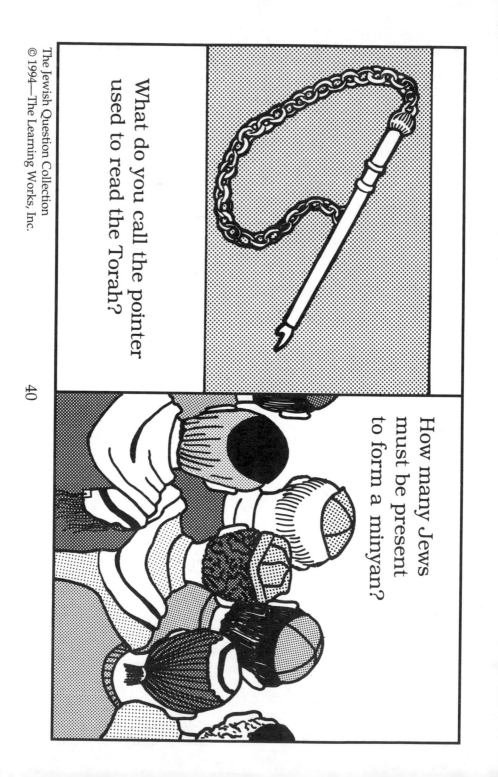

What do you call the pointer used to read the Torah?

How many Jews must be present to form a minyan?

In English,
what is the first word
of the Shema?

שמע

What do you call the mixture
of chopped apples, nuts, and
wine eaten at a Passover seder?

The Jewish Question Collection
© 1994—The Learning Works, Inc.

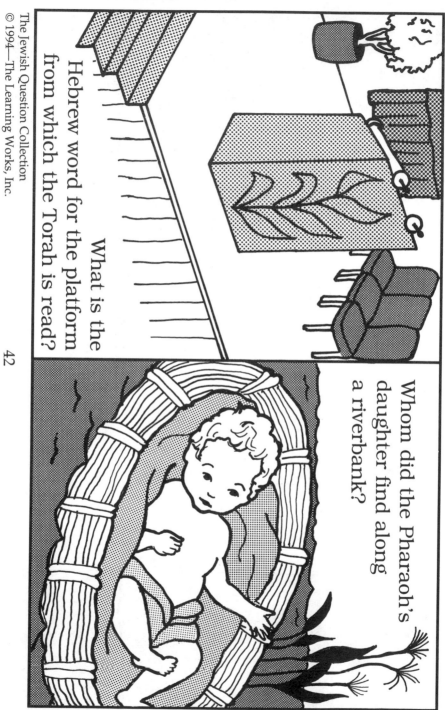

What is the Hebrew word for the platform from which the Torah is read?

Whom did the Pharaoh's daughter find along a riverbank?

The Jewish Question Collection

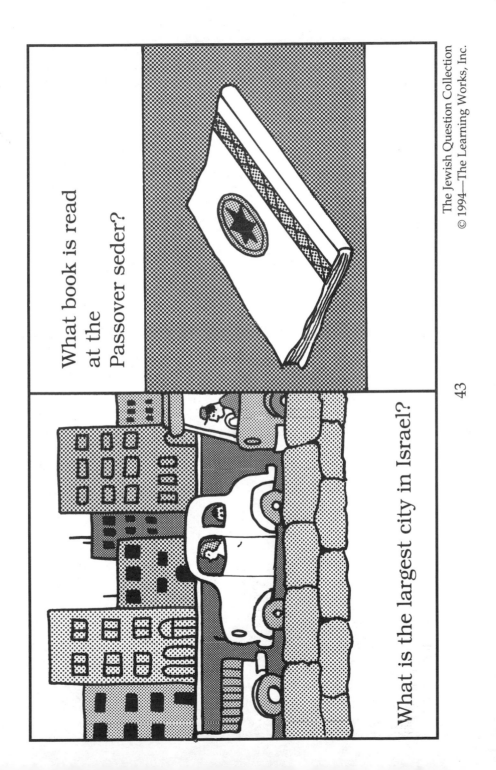

What book is read at the Passover seder?

What is the largest city in Israel?

43

The Jewish Question Collection
© 1994—The Learning Works, Inc.

On what holiday do Jews celebrate the ending and the beginning of the reading of the Torah?

According to the Torah, on which day was light created on Earth?

How many Hebrew words
make up
the Shema?

Shema

Shavua-Tov

What is the meaning of
Shavua-Tov, the greeting
exchanged at the close
of the Havdalah service?

45

In the Bible, which two cities
were destroyed because
the citizens were wicked?

What word
is said
after
a blessing?

46

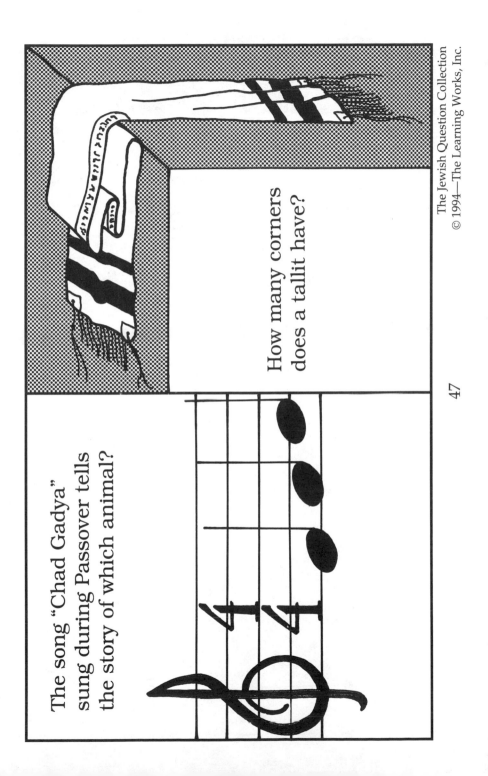

The song "Chad Gadya" sung during Passover tells the story of which animal?

How many corners does a tallit have?

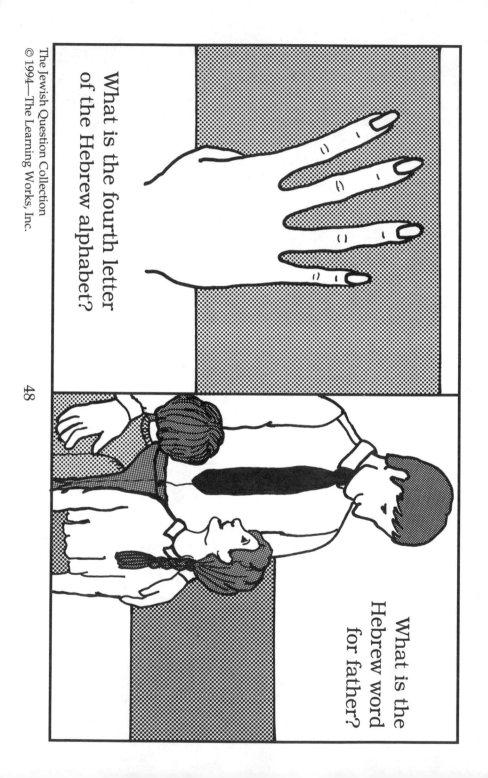

What is the fourth letter
of the Hebrew alphabet?

What is the
Hebrew word
for father?

What is the
Hebrew word
for mother?

Which singer, musician, and creator of psalms was also the second king of Israel?

The Jewish Question Collection
© 1994—The Learning Works, Inc.

Near the end
of the Passover seder,
for whom is a door opened?

How many stars must appear in
the sky as a sign that Shabbat
has ended?

Who was Moses's sister?

What does *Mazel Tov* mean?

The Jewish Question Collection
© 1994—The Learning Works, Inc.

Who had a dream about a ladder that reached up to heaven?

When is the *motzi* recited?

The Jewish Question Collection

52

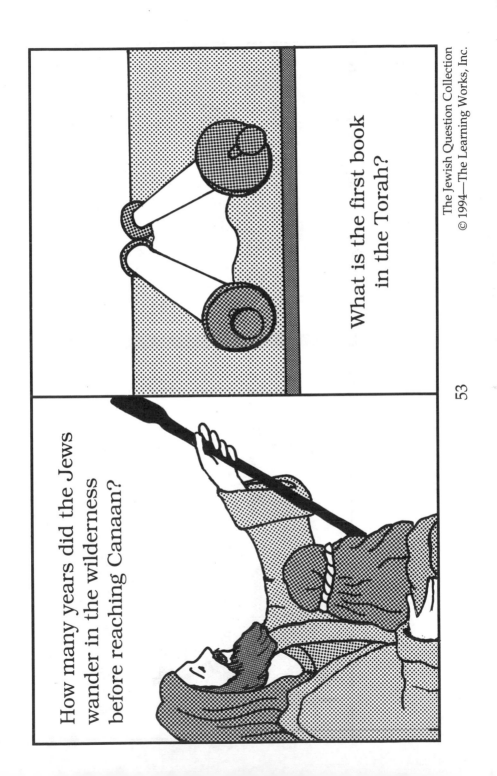

How many years did the Jews wander in the wilderness before reaching Canaan?

What is the first book in the Torah?

The Jewish Question Collection
© 1994—The Learning Works, Inc.

Who murdered Abel?

What is the name of a collective community in Israel where people combine their labor and share property?

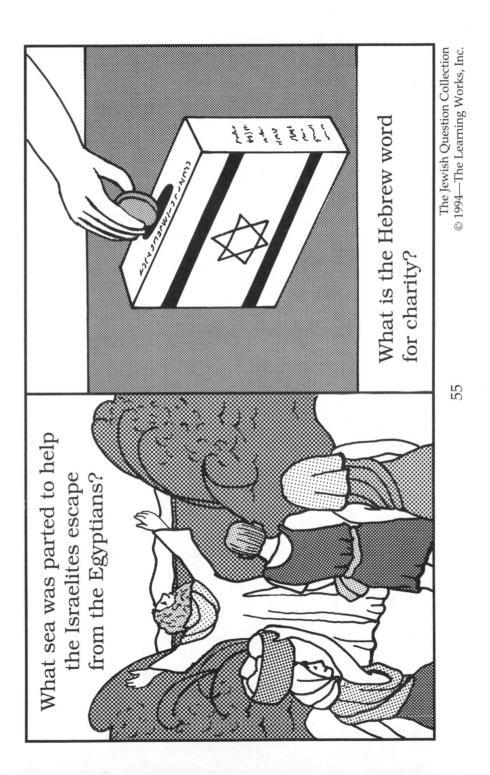

What is the Hebrew word
for charity?

What sea was parted to help
the Israelites escape
from the Egyptians?

The Jewish Question Collection
© 1994—The Learning Works, Inc.

What does the word *afikoman*, the middle matzah, mean?

Whose faith in G–d saved him when he was thrown into a den of lions?

What does the word
rabbi mean?

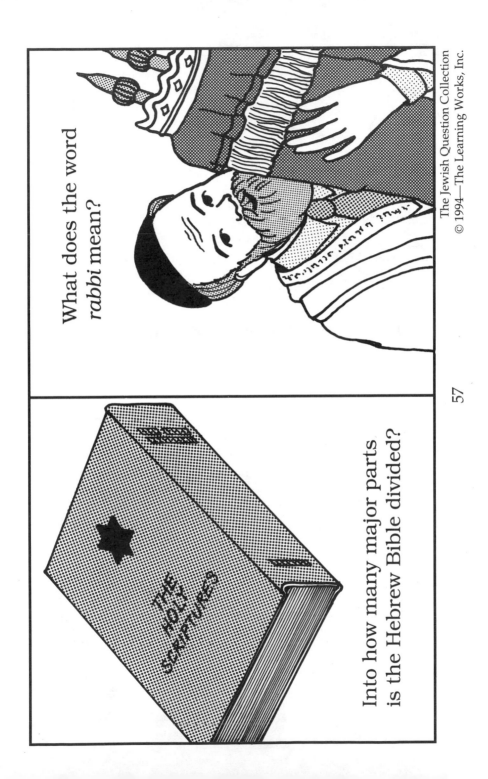

Into how many major parts
is the Hebrew Bible divided?

The Jewish Question Collection
© 1994—The Learning Works, Inc.

Who was King Ahasuerus's
cruel prime minister?

In what year did Israel
become a state?

1950
1953 1945
1948 1947 1949
1951

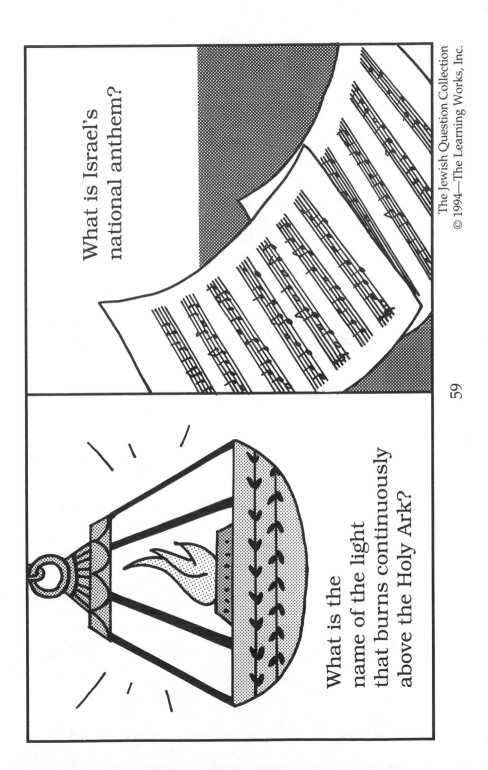

What is Israel's national anthem?

What is the name of the light that burns continuously above the Holy Ark?

In the Book of Genesis,
whose wife turned into
a pillar of salt?

In what city can
the Western Wall be found?

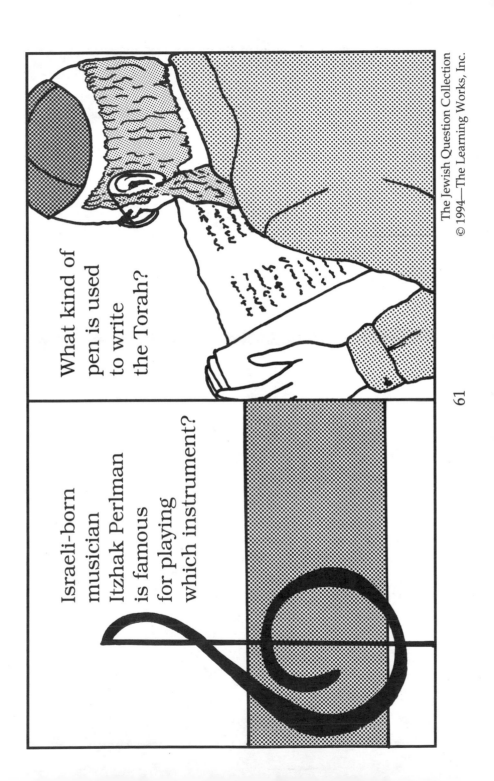

What kind of pen is used to write the Torah?

Israeli-born musician Itzhak Perlman is famous for playing which instrument?

The Jewish Question Collection
© 1994—The Learning Works, Inc.

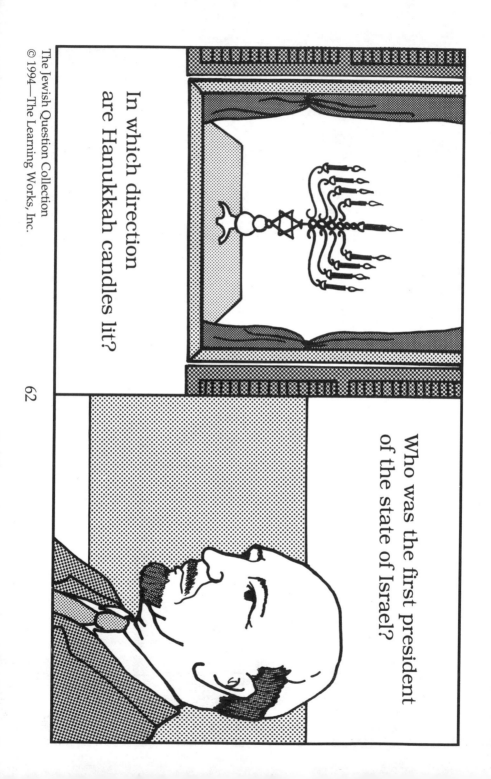

In which direction
are Hanukkah candles lit?

Who was the first president
of the state of Israel?

What is the word for
the seven days
of mourning after a funeral?

During the Holocaust,
who wrote a diary while hidden
in an attic in Holland?

63

The Jewish Question Collection
© 1994—The Learning Works, Inc.

Which prophet's
name begins
with the letter **I**?

What is the word
for the leather boxes
and straps that many
Orthodox Jews
wear in morning prayer?

ALIYAH

What does
the word *aliyah* mean?

"Who asked, "...am I
my brother's keeper?""

The Jewish Question Collection
© 1994—The Learning Works, Inc.

What are the four main branches of Judaism?

What is the word for the ornament on top of a Torah?

Which ancient
Biblical manuscripts
were discovered in 1947
in earthen jars
found in the Judean desert?

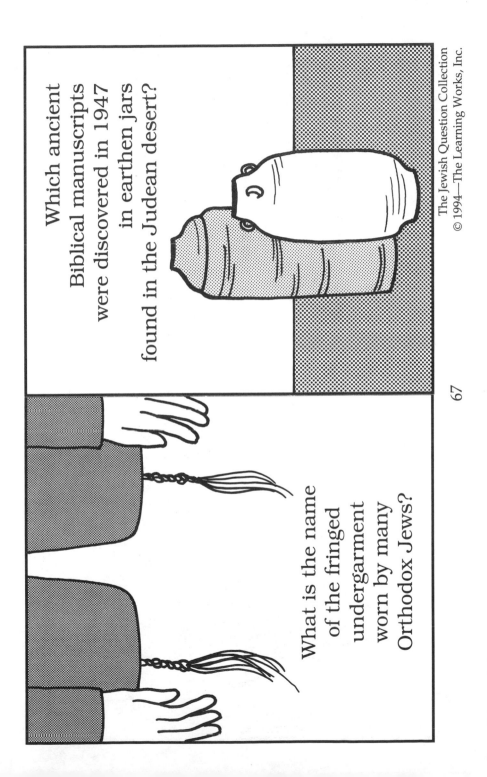

What is the name
of the fringed
undergarment
worn by many
Orthodox Jews?

The Jewish Question Collection
© 1994—The Learning Works, Inc.

What is the Hebrew name
given to a Jewish prayer book?

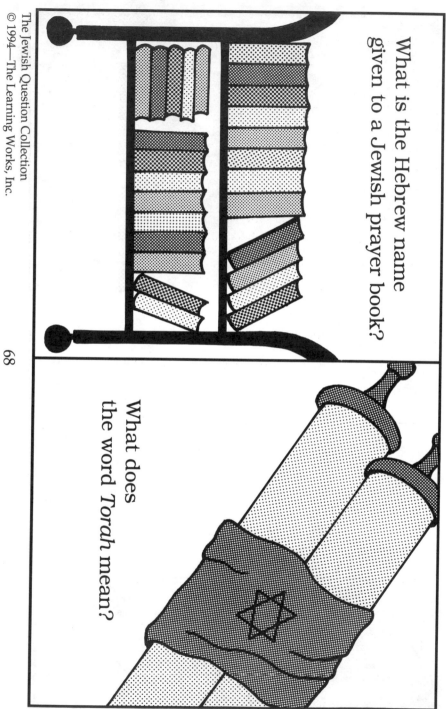

What does
the word *Torah* mean?

Who was the first Jewish manufacturer to make his fortune by creating blue jeans?

What is the Hebrew word for the canopy used in marriage ceremonies?

69

How many mistakes
is a scribe allowed to make
when writing a Torah?

What was the name
of the Assyrian king who
wouldn't allow the Jews
to observe their religion?

Which color is often worn on Yom Kippur as a sign of purity?

What is the special candle lit on the anniversary of a person's death?

The Jewish Question Collection
© 1994—The Learning Works, Inc.

What is kept
inside tefillin?

How many days
after birth
are Jewish boys
circumcised?

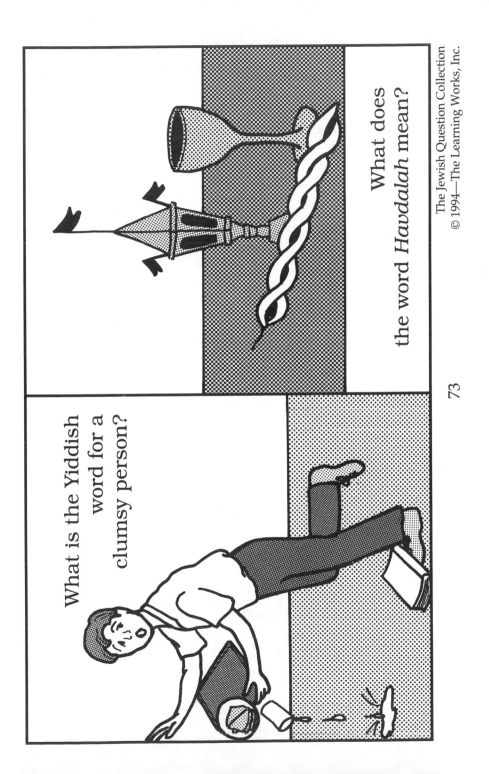

What is the Yiddish
word for a
clumsy person?

What does
the word *Havdalah* mean?

73

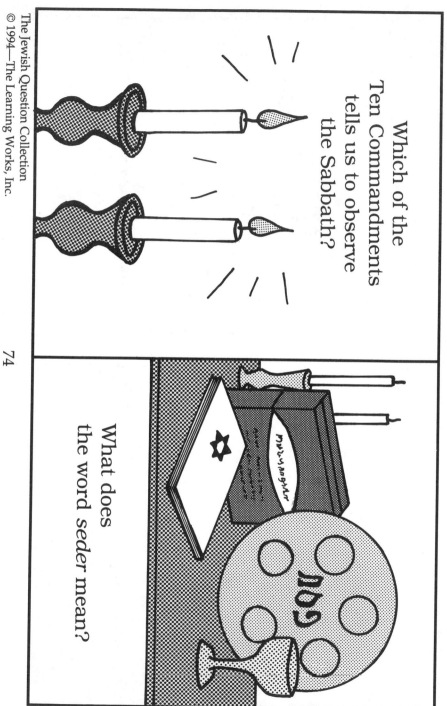

Which of the
Ten Commandments
tells us to observe
the Sabbath?

What does
the word *seder* mean?

What body of water
is directly south of Israel?

The Jewish Question Collection
© 1994—The Learning Works, Inc.

Which woman was
chosen to be
prime minister
of Israel at the
age of seventy?

What is another name for the Five Books of Moses?

On the seder plate, which food symbolizes the new life that comes each spring?

Who was the left-handed pitcher who refused to pitch a World Series game on Yom Kippur?

What was the name of the group of Hebrew soldiers who fought the Assyrians?

The Jewish Question Collection
© 1994—The Learning Works, Inc.

What is the name
of the largest airport in Israel?

What is the English name
for a *chazan*?

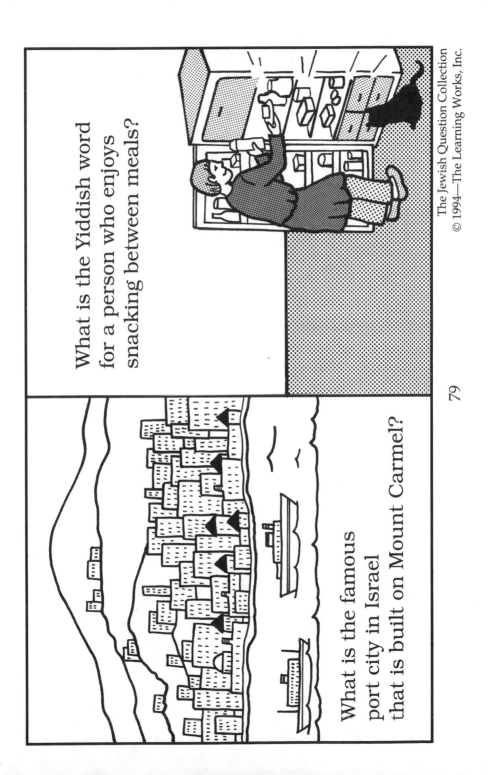

What is the Yiddish word for a person who enjoys snacking between meals?

What is the famous port city in Israel that is built on Mount Carmel?

The Jewish Question Collection
© 1994—The Learning Works, Inc.

What is the Jewish prayer that mourners recite which praises G–d but does not mention death?

The Jewish Question Collection
© 1994—The Learning Works, Inc.

What citrus fruit that resembles a large lemon is used during the holiday of Sukkot?

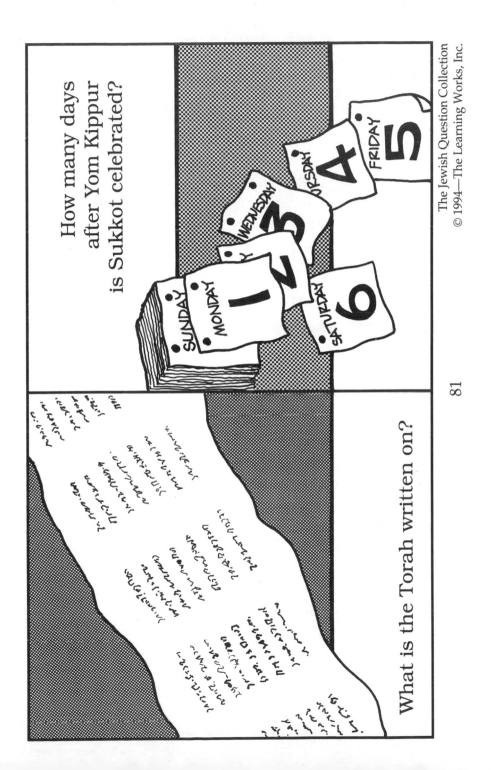

How many days
after Yom Kippur
is Sukkot celebrated?

What is the Torah written on?

Who was the son
of Mattathias
who led the fight
against the
Assyrians?

How old was Sarah
when Isaac was born?

What is the name given to the Nazi persecution and murder of six million European Jews?

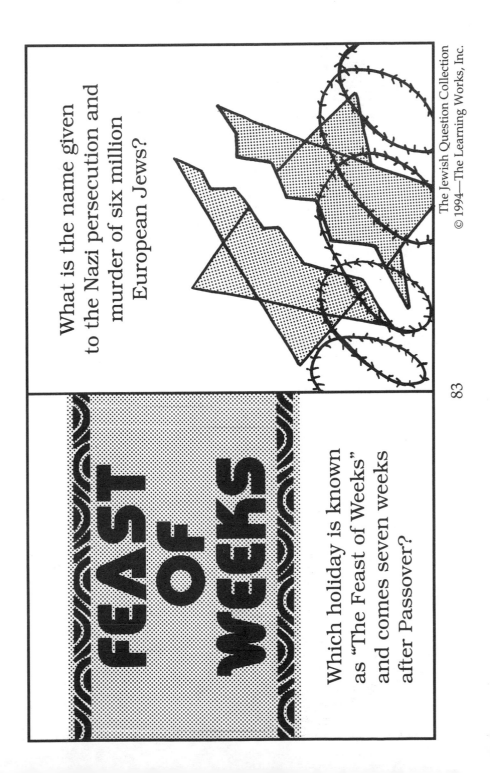

FEAST OF WEEKS

Which holiday is known as "The Feast of Weeks" and comes seven weeks after Passover?

The Jewish Question Collection
© 1994—The Learning Works, Inc.

What Hebrew name, derived from a word meaning "cactus fruit," is given to a native-born Israeli?

What is the Parliament of Israel called?

On which holiday may *chametz* not be eaten?

Who was Abraham's wife and Isaac's mother?

The Jewish Question Collection
© 1994—The Learning Works, Inc.

Dr. Jonas Salk developed a vaccine against what crippling disease?

Which holiday, celebrated in the Jewish month of Kislev, means "dedication"?

On which Jewish holiday
is Confirmation usually held?

What is the English name
for the song "Ma'oz Tzur,"
usually sung during Hanukkah?

The Jewish Question Collection
© 1994—The Learning Works, Inc.

The Yom Kippur service begins with the chanting of what prayer?

In what city is the Hadassah-Hebrew University Medical Center located?

מגן דויד (מגן) אדום(!)

The Jewish Question Collection
© 1994—The Learning Works, Inc.

What do the four letters
on a dreidel stand for?

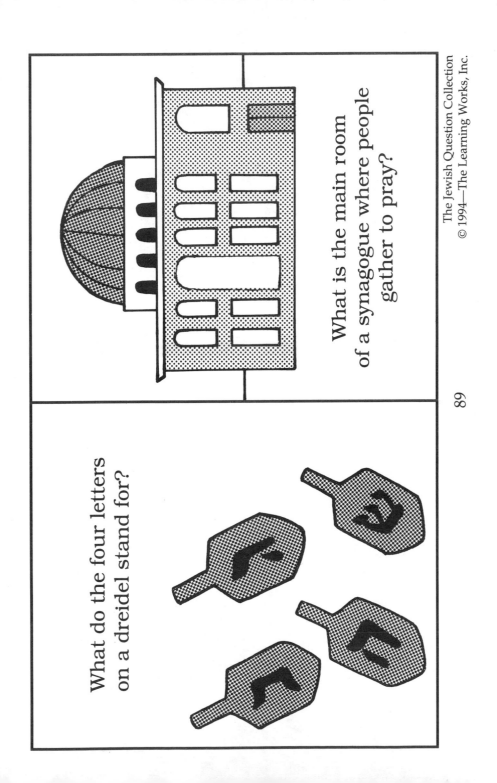

What is the main room
of a synagogue where people
gather to pray?

The Jewish Question Collection
© 1994—The Learning Works, Inc.

Which way should the top of a mezuzah slant when hung on a doorpost?

What is the name of the palm branch used during Sukkot?

What German-born Jewish physicist won the Nobel Prize for his Theory of Relativity?

What is Israel's official memorial for the victims of the Holocaust?

Nes Gadol Hayah Sham

What do the words *Nes Gadol Hayah Sham* mean?

On which Jewish holiday do people plant trees?

How many blessings are recited when a mezuzah is hung on a doorpost?

Which body of water borders the western coast of Israel?

The Jewish Question Collection
© 1994—The Learning Works, Inc.

According to tradition, who wrote the Twenty-Third Psalm?

Which holiday is celebrated on the thirty-third day of the counting of omer, between Passover and Shavuot?

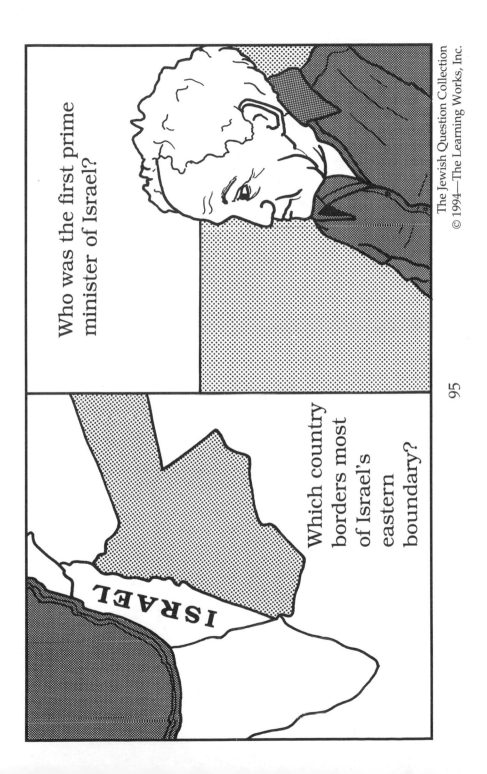

Who was the first prime minister of Israel?

Which country borders most of Israel's eastern boundary?

ISRAEL

The Jewish Question Collection
© 1994—The Learning Works, Inc.

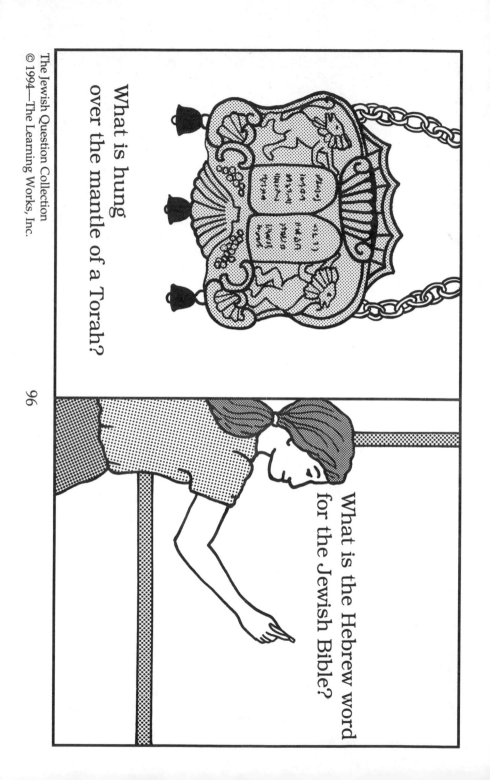

What is hung over the mantle of a Torah?

What is the Hebrew word for the Jewish Bible?

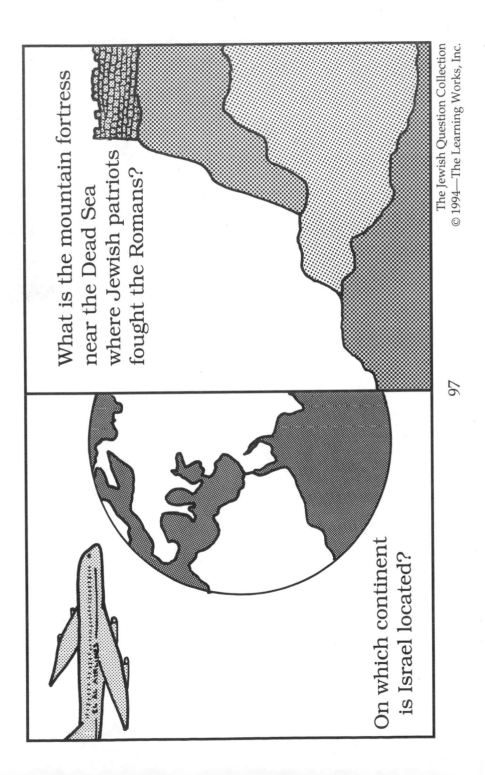

What is the mountain fortress near the Dead Sea where Jewish patriots fought the Romans?

On which continent is Israel located?

97

Which holiday is celebrated
with parties and parades
in honor of Israel's
independence?

What is the difference
between an American
and an Israeli dreidel?

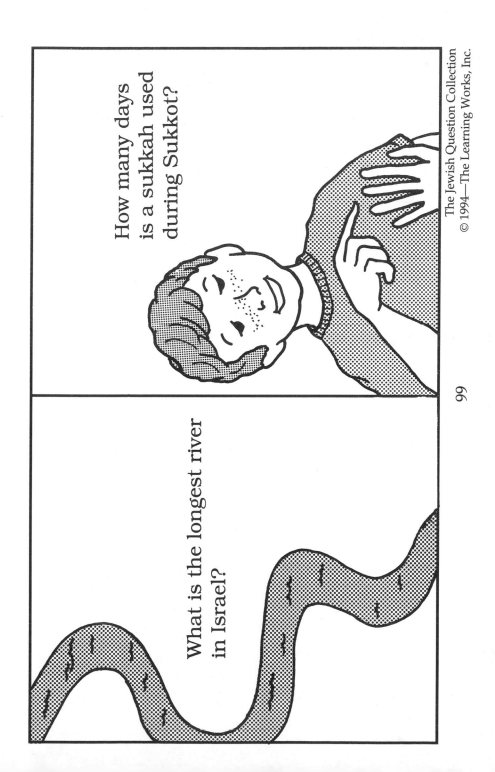

What is the longest river in Israel?

How many days is a sukkah used during Sukkot?

99

Who was
the military hero
who wore
an eyepatch
and was famous
for leading
the Sinai Campaign?

How many
cups of wine
should each person
drink during
the seder?

In which book of the Bible is the story of Purim found?

How many sons did Jacob have?

101

The Jewish Question Collection
© 1994—The Learning Works, Inc.

What is the first note
the shofar sounds
on Rosh Hashanah?

The ancient walls
of which city fell down
when Joshua shouted
and people blew shofars?

1ST KING

Who was the first king of the Israelites?

What famous tower was started but never finished because the people couldn't understand each other?

The Jewish Question Collection
© 1994—The Learning Works, Inc.

Who was King Ahasuerus's first queen?

Who is the Russian-born artist famous for creating the design for the stained glass windows of the Hadassah Hospital?

In the story of Purim, what did Mordechai refuse to do to Haman?

What war did Israel fight and win against Jordan, Syria, and Egypt in June, 1967?

The Jewish Question Collection
© 1994—The Learning Works, Inc.

On which holiday is it customary to eat dairy foods?

According to tradition, how many mitzvot are in the Torah?

Who was the founder of
the Zionist movement and
the author of *The Jewish State?*

The Jewish Question Collection
© 1994—The Learning Works, Inc.

The story of Purim
takes place in Persia.
What is Persia
called today?

Before the establishment of Israel, what was the defense force of the Jews in Palestine called?

How many letters are found in the basic Hebrew alphabet?

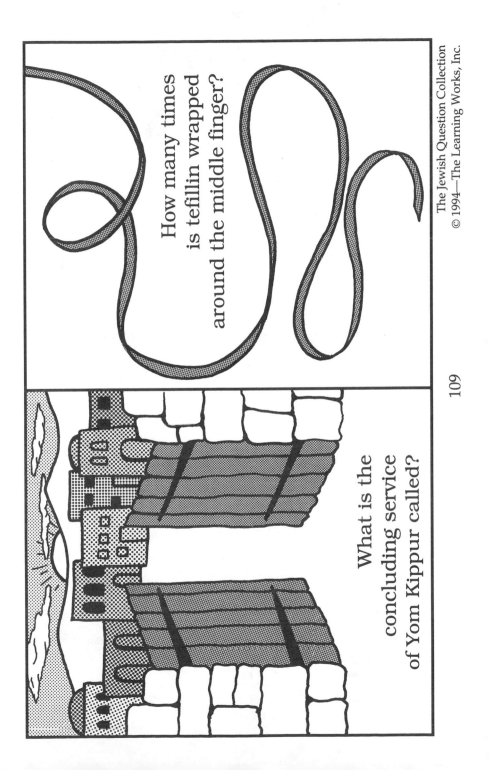

How many times
is tefillin wrapped
around the middle finger?

What is the
concluding service
of Yom Kippur called?

109

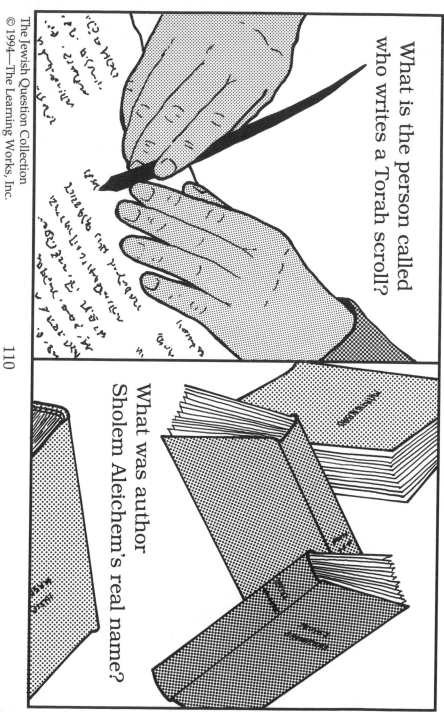

What is the person called
who writes a Torah scroll?

What was author
Sholem Aleichem's real name?

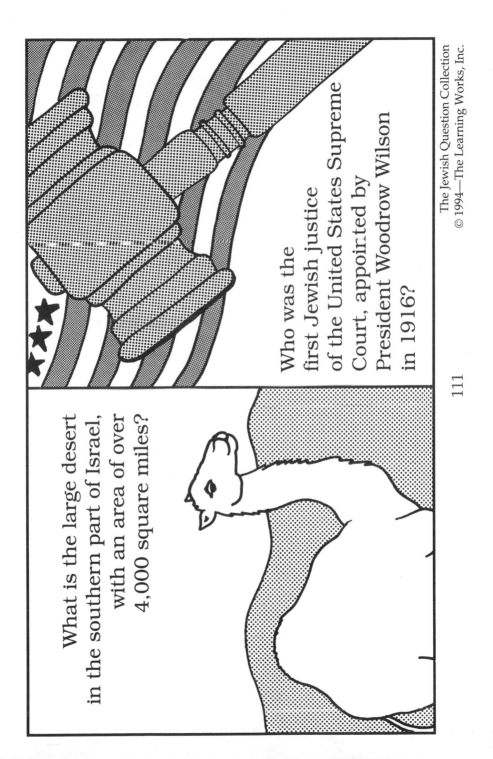

Who was the
first Jewish justice
of the United States Supreme
Court, appointed by
President Woodrow Wilson
in 1916?

What is the large desert
in the southern part of Israel,
with an area of over
4,000 square miles?

The Jewish Question Collection
© 1994—The Learning Works, Inc.

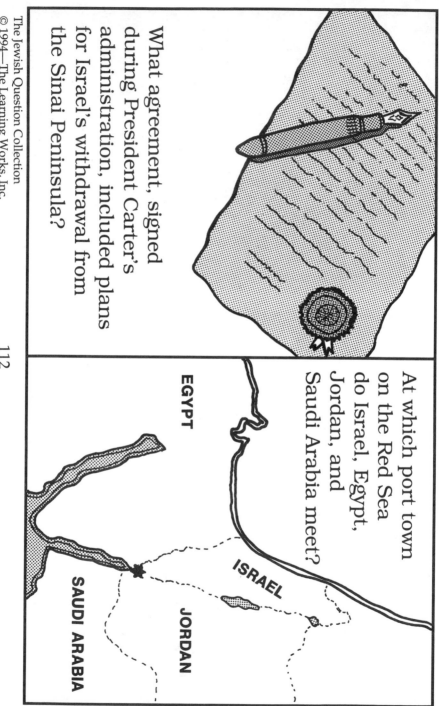

What agreement, signed during President Carter's administration, included plans for Israel's withdrawal from the Sinai Peninsula?

At which port town on the Red Sea do Israel, Egypt, Jordan, and Saudi Arabia meet?

EGYPT

ISRAEL

JORDAN

SAUDI ARABIA

Who succeeded Menachem Begin as Prime Minister of Israel in 1983?

How many daughters did Tevye have in the movie and play *Fiddler on the Roof?*

The Jewish Question Collection
© 1994—The Learning Works, Inc.

Who was the famous rabbi and scholar who urged the Jews to rebel against the Romans?

Where is the tomb of the Patriarchs located?

The Jewish Question Collection
© 1994—The Learning Works, Inc.

Who was the founder of Hadassah, the Women's Zionist Organization of America?

Who was the first American scientist to win a Nobel Prize in physics in 1907?

Which American Jewish poet wrote the sonnet "The New Colossus," which can be found on the Statue of Liberty?

What book in the Bible comes after Psalms?

תהילים
PSALMS

What book by Lois Lowry won the 1990 Newbery Award and told the story of Jewish people saved by Danes during the Holocaust?

What is the Yiddish word for a small, Jewish community in Eastern Europe that made up all or part of a village?

Which Roman emperor wouldn't allow Jews to study the Torah?

How many prophets are there in the Book of Prophets?

The Jewish Question Collection
© 1994—The Learning Works, Inc.

SYRIA

Golan Heights

River Jordan

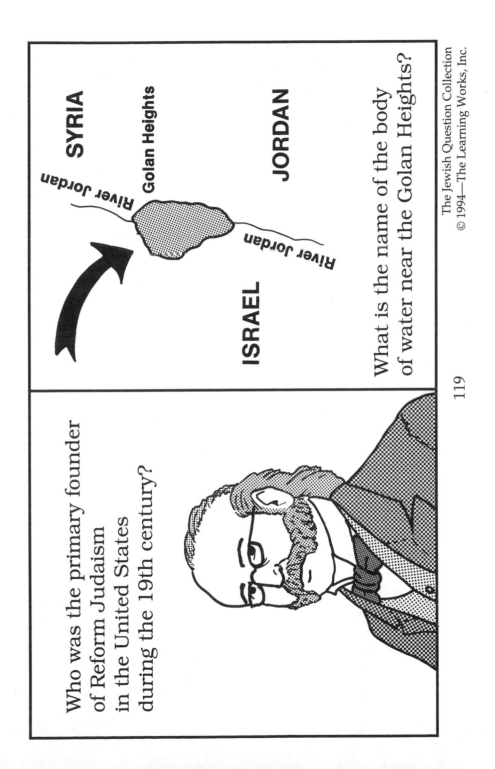

ISRAEL

River Jordan

JORDAN

What is the name of the body
of water near the Golan Heights?

The Jewish Question Collection
© 1994—The Learning Works, Inc.

119

Who was the primary founder
of Reform Judaism
in the United States
during the 19th century?

Who played the role of a cantor's son in the first talking picture, *The Jazz Singer*?

Which person in the Bible was also known as Israel?

How many members make up
Israel's Parliament?

What is the first month of the
modern Hebrew calendar?

The Jewish Question Collection
© 1994—The Learning Works, Inc.

What is the final *aliyah* called in any Sabbath morning service?

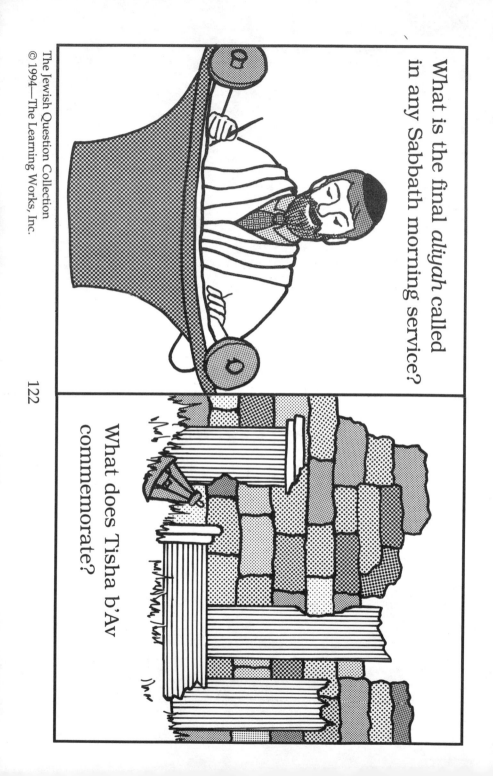

What does Tisha b'Av commemorate?

The Jewish Question Collection

What were the names of Isaac and Rebekah's two sons?

Besides the palm and the etrog, which two plants are symbolic of Sukkot?

The Jewish Question Collection
© 1994—The Learning Works, Inc.

What do you call
the special markings
used to chant the Torah?

שְׁמַע יִשְׂרָאֵל יְיָ
אֱלֹהֵינוּ יְיָ
אֶחָד׃

What memorial service
for the dead is held on
Yom Kippur, Passover, Shavuot,
and Shemini Atzeret?

The Jewish Question Collection
© 1994—The Learning Works, Inc.

What is the name of the highest mountain in Israel?

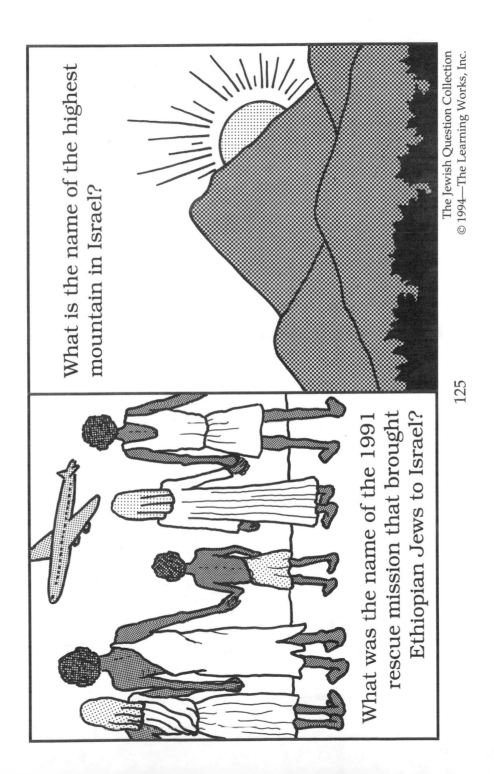

What was the name of the 1991 rescue mission that brought Ethiopian Jews to Israel?

Which one is *not* a fall month:
Tishri, Heshvan, or Nisan?

What was the language
spoken by many Eastern
European Jews?

**Bei mir bist
du schoen!**

Which one is *not*
a summer month: Tammuz,
Adar, Av, or Elul?

Who produced and directed the
movie *Fiddler on the Roof*?

DIRECTOR

The Jewish Question Collection
© 1994—The Learning Works, Inc.

How many psalms are found in the Hebrew Bible?

Does *bikkur holim* refer to celebrating spring, visiting the sick, or cooking a kosher meal?

Who succeeded Moses
and led the Jewish people
back to Canaan?

ba'al tekiah

What is a *ba'al tekiah*
skilled at doing?

The Jewish Question Collection
© 1994—The Learning Works, Inc.

Which section of an evening or morning service is read standing up and in silence?

According to the Bible, how old was Abraham when he died?

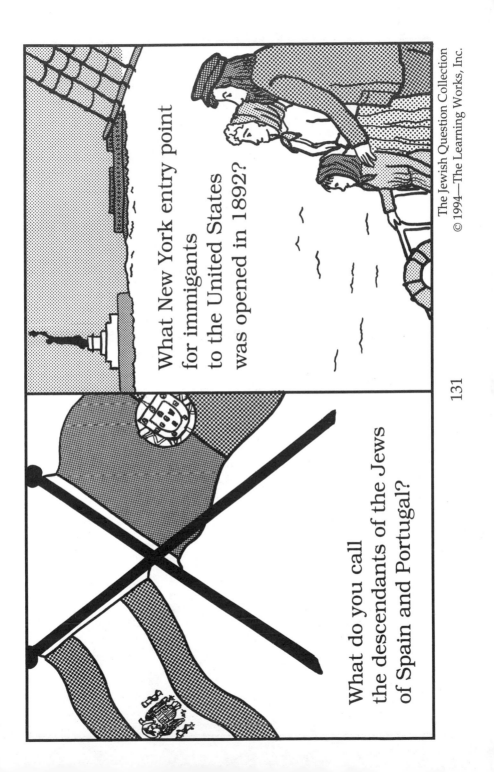

What New York entry point
for immigrants
to the United States
was opened in 1892?

What do you call
the descendants of the Jews
of Spain and Portugal?

The Jewish Question Collection
© 1994—The Learning Works, Inc.

What do you call
the descendants of the Jews
of eastern and central Europe?

What are the two
official languages of Israel?

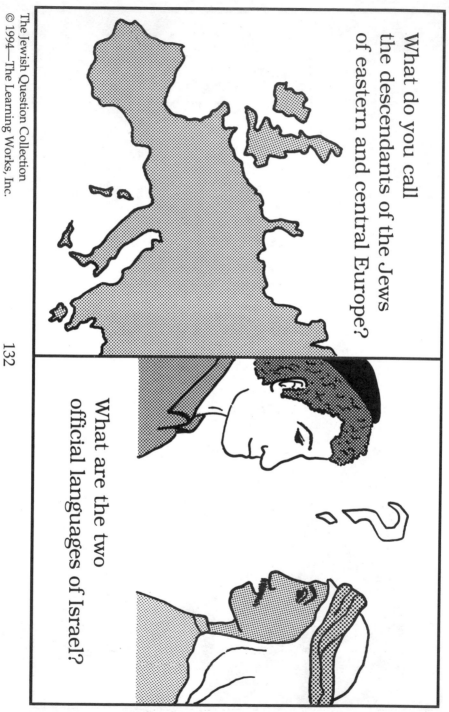

What is the name of the document that announced Great Britain's support for the creation of a Jewish homeland in Palestine?

Which university, founded in 1948 in Massachusetts, was the first Jewish-sponsored nonsectarian school in the United States?

Which book of the Bible is read during Shavuot?

Who was the director of the Los Alamos project, which gave America the atom bomb?

100 60 76 88 65 68 99 32 18 24 70 57 47

The Torah is divided into how many portions?

What is the name of the Polish Jew who founded the Hasidic movement?

The Jewish Question Collection
© 1994—The Learning Works, Inc.

The Jewish Question Collection
© 1994—The Learning Works, Inc.

I   II   III

IV   V   VI

Which of the Ten
Commandments says
"Thou shalt not steal"?

VII   VIII

IX   X

What was the name of
Joseph's youngest brother?

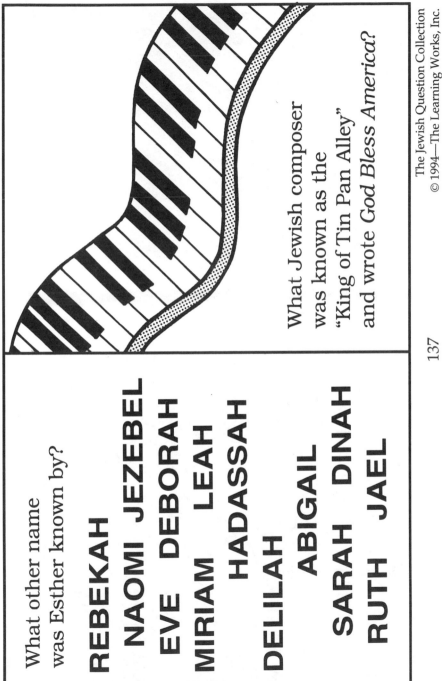

What Jewish composer
was known as the
"King of Tin Pan Alley"
and wrote *God Bless America?*

The Jewish Question Collection
© 1994—The Learning Works, Inc.

What other name
was Esther known by?

**REBEKAH
NAOMI JEZEBEL
EVE DEBORAH
MIRIAM LEAH
HADASSAH
DELILAH
ABIGAIL
SARAH DINAH
RUTH JAEL**

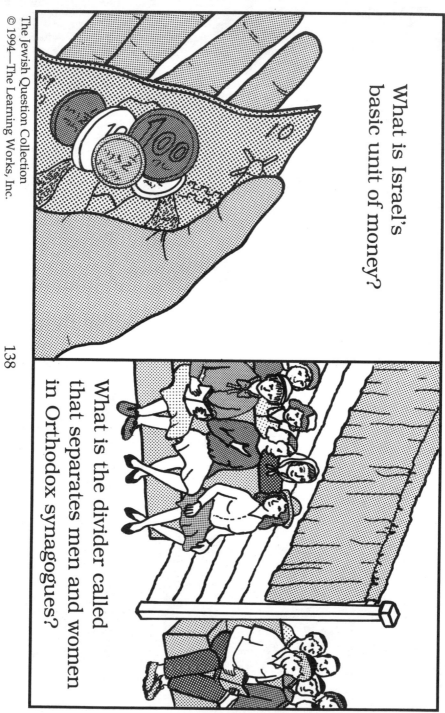

What is Israel's basic unit of money?

What is the divider called that separates men and women in Orthodox synagogues?

The Jewish Question Collection

What was the name
of Adam and Eve's third son?

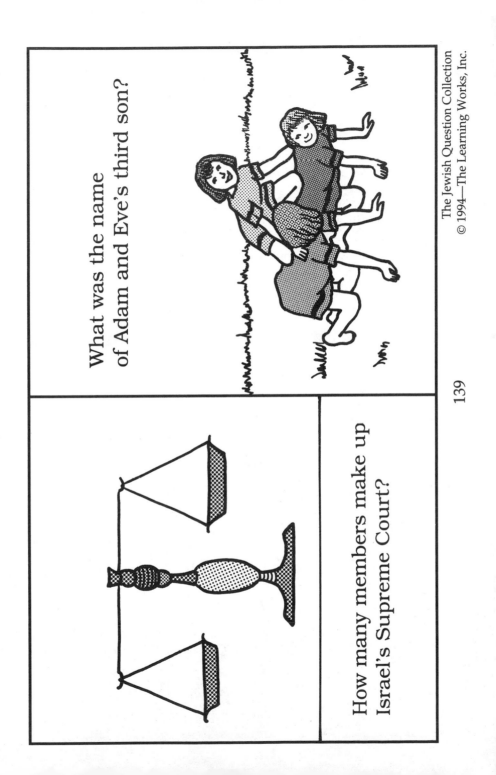

How many members make up
Israel's Supreme Court?

The Jewish Question Collection
© 1994—The Learning Works, Inc.

What was
the name of
Moses's wife?

In 1993, which Jewish woman
did President Bill Clinton
appoint to the
U.S. Supreme Court?

What is the Judeo-Spanish dialect used by Sephardic Jews?

Who was the French-Jewish captain accused of the sale of secret documents to Germany?

141

What was the massacre of Jews, especially in Russia and other Eastern European countries, called?

What is the Hebrew word for the ritual bath of purification?

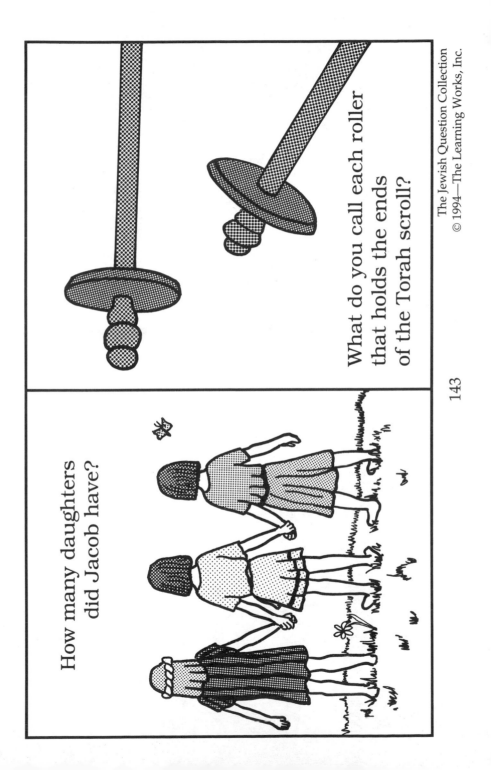

What do you call each roller that holds the ends of the Torah scroll?

How many daughters did Jacob have?

The Jewish Question Collection
© 1994—The Learning Works, Inc.

Who was king during
the building of the First Temple
in Jerusalem?

What does
the word *kosher* mean?

BEANS

GELATIN K

RICE NOODLES

GEFILTE FISH

In what year did
the Sinai Campaign take place?

What is the
cloth that covers
the Torah called?

What is the name for the curls worn by Hasidic males?

Which nation ruled Israel immediately after World War I?

United States

Spain

Fra

The Jewish Question Collection

146

What is the name of academies of Jewish learning where students study Jewish law and custom?

In what year was Israel admitted to the United Nations?

147

What was the relationship between Ruth and Naomi?

How many sections does the Talmud contain?

148

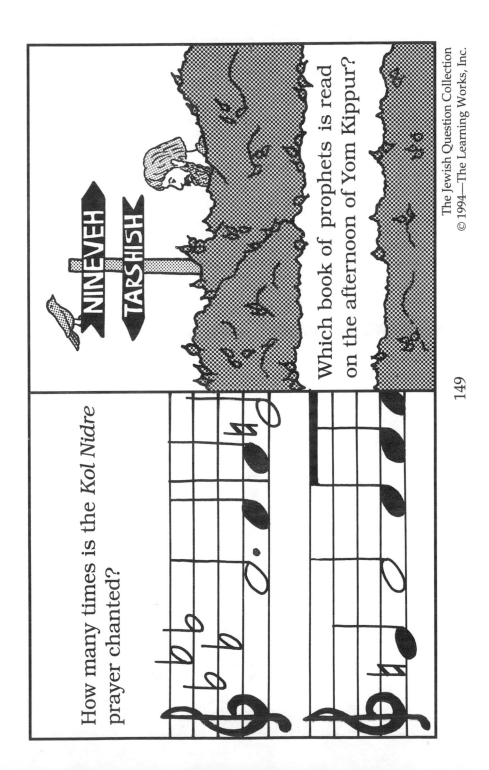

Which book of prophets is read on the afternoon of Yom Kippur?

How many times is the *Kol Nidre* prayer chanted?

149

What is the name
of the Jewish marriage contract
that is written in Aramaic?

Which of the Ten
Commandments states
"Thou shalt have no other gods
before me?"

In which country did the first World Zionist Congress meet?

What was the name of Abraham's servant who arranged the marriage of Isaac and Rebekah?

Have I got a match for you!

What is the Hebrew term
for a Jewish bill of divorce?

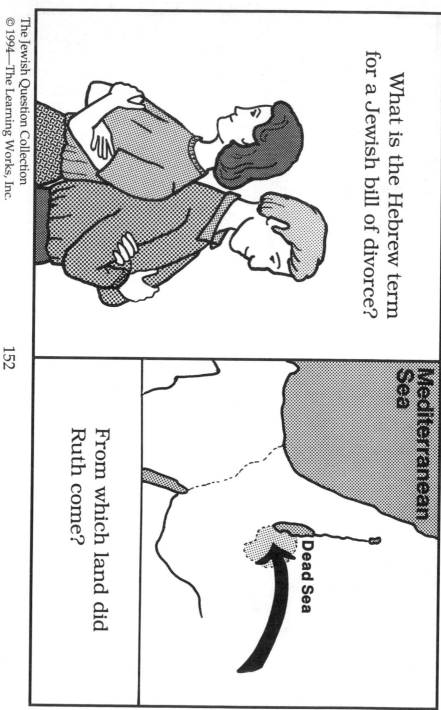

From which land did
Ruth come?

Mediterranean
Sea

Dead Sea

152

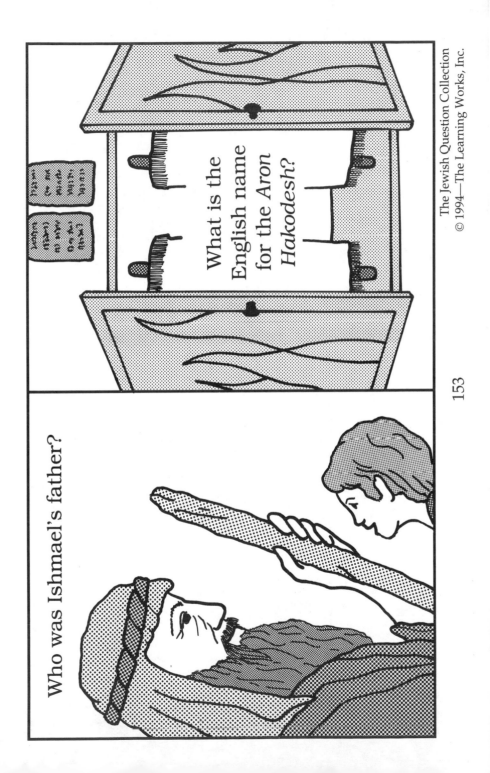

Who was Ishmael's father?

What is the English name for the Aron Hakodesh?

In which country was the first matzah-baking machine invented in 1857?

What orator, writer, and militant Zionist became the first president of Israel's Herut Party?

On Rosh Hashanah, what is the name of the afternoon service that takes place by a river or flowing stream?

What is the name of the prayer service said each morning?

The Jewish Question Collection
© 1994—The Learning Works, Inc.

How old was Anne Frank when she died?

The two passages found on the scroll inside a mezuzah come from which book of the Bible?

Who was the third son
of Jacob and Leah?

FIRST
SECOND
THIRD

What are the names of the three
Patriarchs, or Biblical ancestors,
of the people of Israel?

The Jewish Question Collection
© 1994—The Learning Works, Inc.

Answer Key

Page 7
a. six
b. dreidel

Page 8
a. the Sabbath or Shabbat
b. Rosh Hashanah

Page 9
a. eight
b. Kiddush

Page 10
a. the shamash
b. the Star of David

Page 11
a. shofar
b. the Garden of Eden

Page 12
a. kippot or yarmulkas
b. Yom Kippur

Page 13
a. matzah
b. six

Page 14
a. hamantashen
b. shalom

Page 15
a. blue and white
b. Noah

Page 16
a. challah
b. Bat or Bas Mitzvah

Page 17
a. Jonah
b. the Ark

Page 18
a. Purim
b. David

Page 19
a. right
b. potatoes

Page 20
a. dietary laws
b. Purim

Page 21
a. ten
b. Moses

Page 22
a. Passover or Pesach
b. rested

The Jewish Question Collection
© 1994—The Learning Works, Inc.

Page 23
a. thirteen
b. right to left

Page 24
a. the Exodus
b. Sukkot

Page 25
a. four
b. a prayer shawl

Page 26
a. aleph
b. Abraham

Page 27
a. a dove
b. Passover or Pesach

Page 28
a. Abraham
b. the lighting of the candles

Page 29
a. Cain
b. to show respect

Page 30
a. Mount Sinai
b. a year

Page 31
a. Samson
b. Joseph

Page 32
a. a roasted lamb bone or zeroa
b. Purim

Page 33
a. hanukkiah
b. honey

Page 34
a. to remember the tears Jews shed
   as slaves in Egypt
b. Abel

Page 35
a. Confirmation
b. bet

Page 36
a. menorahs
b. Jerusalem

Page 37
a. horseradish or maror
b. The player gets half the pot.

Page 38
a. the minimum number of adult
   Jews required to hold a public
   worship service
b. the Dead Sea

Page 39

a. written by hand

b. eat

Page 40

a. a yad

b. ten

Page 41

a. haroset

b. Hear

Page 42

a. bimah

b. Moses

Page 43

a. Tel Aviv

b. the Haggadah

Page 44

a. Simchat Torah

b. the first

Page 45

a. a good week

b. six

Page 46

a. Sodom and Gomorrah

b. Amen

Page 47
a. a baby goat or kid
b. four

Page 48
a. dalet
b. abba

Page 49
a. King David
b. ima

Page 50
a. Elijah
b. three

Page 51
a. Miriam
b. congratulations, good luck

Page 52
a. Jacob
b. any time bread is eaten

Page 53
a. forty years
b. Genesis or Bereshit

Page 54
a. Cain
b. a kibbutz

Page 55

a. the Red Sea or Sea of Reeds

b. *tzedakah*

Page 56

a. dessert or entertainment

b. Daniel

Page 57

a. three

b. teacher

Page 58

a. Haman

b. 1948

Page 59

a. the Eternal Light or Ner Tamid

b. *Hatikvah*

Page 60

a. Lot's

b. Jerusalem

Page 61

a. the violin

b. a feather pen or quill

Page 62

a. left to right

b. Chaim Weizmann

Page 63
a. Anne Frank
b. shivah

Page 64
a. Isaiah
b. tefillin or phylacteries

Page 65
a. Cain
b. going up

Page 66
a. Orthodox, Conservative,
   Reconstructionist, and Reform
b. a crown, keter, or rimonim

Page 67
a. talit katan
b. the Dead Sea Scrolls

Page 68
a. Siddur
b. teaching or law

Page 69
a. chupa
b. Levi Strauss

Page 70
a. none
b. Antiochus

The Jewish Question Collection
© 1994—The Learning Works, Inc.

Page 71

a. a memorial candle or yahrzeit

b. white

Page 72

a. scrolls written with verses from the Torah

b. seven days after birth, on the eighth day of life

Page 73

a. a klutz

b. separation or division

Page 74

a. the fourth

b. order

Page 75

a. Golda Meir

b. the Red Sea

Page 76

a. Torah

b. a roasted egg or betzah

Page 77

a. the Maccabees

b. Sandy Koufax

Page 78

a. Lod

b. a cantor

The Jewish Question Collection
© 1994—The Learning Works, Inc.

Page 79
a. Haifa
b. nosher

Page 80
a. the Kaddish
b. the etrog

Page 81
a. parchment or leather
b. five

Page 82
a. Judah the Maccabee
b. ninety years old

Page 83
a. Shavuot
b. the Holocaust

Page 84
a. sabra
b. the Knesset

Page 85
a. Sarah
b. Passover or Pesach

Page 86
a. polio
b. Hanukkah

The Jewish Question Collection
© 1994—The Learning Works, Inc.

Page 87

a. "Rock of Ages"

b. Shavuot

Page 88

a. Jerusalem

b. Kol Nidre

Page 89

a. *Nes Gadol Hayah Sham*

b. the sanctuary

Page 90

a. toward the inside of the house or room

b. a lulav

Page 91

a. Yad Vashem

b. Albert Einstein

Page 92

a. "A great miracle happened there."

b. Tu b'Shevat

Page 93

a. two

b. the Mediterranean Sea

Page 94

a. King David

b. Lag Ba-Omer

Page 95
a. Jordan
b. David Ben-Gurion

Page 96
a. a breastplate
b. Tanakh

Page 97
a. Asia
b. Masada

Page 98
a. Yom Ha-Atzma'ut
b. The letter "pay" which stands for "here" appears on an Israeli dreidel and the letter "shin" which stands for "there" appears on an American dreidel.

Page 99
a. the River Jordan
b. seven or eight

Page 100
a. Moshe Dayan
b. four

Page 101
a. the Book of Esther
b. twelve

Page 102
a. tekiah
b. Jericho

169

The Jewish Question Collection
© 1994—The Learning Works, Inc.

Page 103
a. the Tower of Babel
b. Saul

Page 104
a. Vashti
b. Marc Chagall

Page 105
a. the Six-Day War
b. bow down to him

Page 106
a. Shavuot
b. 613

Page 107
a. Iran
b. Theodor Herzl

Page 108
a. the Haganah
b. twenty-two

Page 109
a. Neilah
b. seven times

Page 110
a. a sofer or scribe
b. Sholem Rabinowitz

Page 111
a. the Negev
b. Louis Brandeis

Page 112
a. the Camp David Accords
b. Elat

Page 113
a. Yitzhak Shamir
b. five

Page 114
a. Hebron
b. Rabbi Akiba

Page 115
a. Albert Abraham Michelson
b. Henrietta Szold

Page 116
a. Emma Lazarus
b. Proverbs

Page 117
a. shtetl
b. *Number the Stars*

Page 118
a. Hadrian
b. fifteen

Page 119

a. Rabbi Isaac Mayer Wise

b. the Sea of Galilee or Kinneret

Page 120

a. Al Jolson

b. Jacob

Page 121

a. Tishri

b. 120

Page 122

a. maftir

b. the destruction of the first and
   second Temple in Jerusalem

Page 123

a. myrtle and willow

b. Esau and Jacob

Page 124

a. Yizkor

b. trope

Page 125

a. Operation Moses

b. Mount Meron

Page 126

a. Nisan

b. Yiddish

Page 127
a. Harold Prince
b. Adar

Page 128
a. 150
b. visiting the sick

Page 129
a. blowing the shofar
b. Joshua

Page 130
a. the Amidah, Shemoneh Esrei, or Tefilah
b. 175

Page 131
a. Sephardim
b. Ellis Island

Page 132
a. Ashkenazim
b. Hebrew and Arabic

Page 133
a. Brandeis
b. the Balfour Declaration

Page 134
a. the Book of Ruth
b. Dr. J. Robert Oppenheimer

173

Page 135
a. Israel Baal Shem-Tov
b. fifty-four

Page 136
a. the eighth
b. Benjamin

Page 137
a. Hadassah
b. Irving Berlin

Page 138
a. the shekel
b. mechitzah

Page 139
a. ten
b. Seth

Page 140
a. Zipporah
b. Ruth Bader Ginsburg

Page 141
a. Alfred Dreyfus
b. Ladino

Page 142
a. a pogrom
b. mikveh

Page 143
a. one
b. etz chayim

Page 144
a. King Solomon
b. clean, fit, or proper

Page 145
a. a mantle
b. 1956

Page 146
a. payess
b. Great Britain

Page 147
a. 1949
b. yeshivot

Page 148
a. Ruth was Naomi's daughter-in-law.
b. sixty-three

Page 149
a. three
b. the Book of Jonah

Page 150
a. the Ketubah
b. the second

175

Page 151

a. Eliezer

b. Switzerland

Page 152

a. a get

b. Moab

Page 153

a. Abraham

b. the Holy Ark

Page 154

a. Austria

b. Menachem Begin

Page 155

a. the Shacharit

b. Tashlich

Page 156

a. sixteen

b. Deuteronomy

Page 157

a. Abraham, Isaac, and Jacob

b. Levi